Fear Taught The Bird Not To Sing

by Amanda Everwood

CHAPTERS

3

chapter one

for when your wings are
broken

she was the darkest of nights
not afraid of the dark
the world
never saw
her coming

-*the world never saw her coming*

worse than being alone
is feeling alone
with someone
who used
to make you feel

infine

-*infinite*

even in a broken heart
there is the
indomitable
force
of love

-*even in a broken heart*

people treat you
the way
they see
themselves

don't take to heart
what they say

they shout at mirrors
not knowing they are windows

-mirrors and windows

as the night drips
down the faucet
in slow, rhythmic taps

i think of you
and the way
things used to be

-*thinking of you*

i watched you walk
away from me
and found myself
wishing
i was
the ground
beneath your feet

-*anything, anything*

today
it feels
as if
the clouds
will never stop
covering
the sun

-*cloudy day*

i wish for sleep
so that i can exist
without thinking of you

but even here
you haunt me
as i dream of you

-*you haunt me even here*

despite my best intentions
i found myself
thinking of you
again

-*loving you against my will*

i want to seduce you
one last time
make you come back
if only for the night

-if only for one night

oh, the way you affect me
i would be red in the face
if i had to speak of them aloud

-*blush*

sometimes, by letting go
we gain.

-letting go

my mind is a jail cell
that will never
let you out

-the prison is a prisoner

with just a smile
you resurrected
my feelings for you
back from the dead

-just a smile

self hatred
break the mirror

-seven years of bad luck

even in darkness
she never forgot
the light
she truly was

-love by candlelight

i want to travel
all around the world
to art museums

for only like this
can i understand
what life is
and how
it's meant

-to be lived

you make me
fall in love

-*superpower*

most nights, all i can do
is miss you
knowing
i can never
get you
back

-*i miss you*

he may have broken you
but you will rise
beautiful and powerful
from the ashes

-from the ashes

i want to be
needed
by you

-*sexually*

she is
the ocean
in a human soul

the wind
crashing the waves
onto the shore

she is
the moonlit night
of equinox

-equinox

love is waiting
for the right person
at the right time

taking our chances
against all odds
finding love
by grace of god

-*grace of god*

it is so tragic
the way people never seem
to miss you
until you're gone

-*until you're gone*

in reverie
i call out to you
desperate
for a syllable
from your lips
so that at least
my ears
may taste them

-*taste*

broken
you left me
and yet
i still
want you

-i still want you

love is a feeling
i only wish
i could forget

-feeling

chapter two

for when you're afraid to fly

she was a woman
too strong
for most men

they were too weak
to play with fire

-*play with fire*

i've seen the way
you look at me
and i can only hope
we're meant to be

-meant to be

how many bombs
do we have to drop
before we stop repeating
our worst mistake?

-bombs in the sand

you will always be
immortal

engraved forever
in my thoughts

-*tombstone of romance*

our love is forbidden
but that won't stop me
as surely as the night sky
cannot stop
the rising sun

-rising sun

women
should make
as much money
as men

-*full stop.*

awestruck gazes
hidden behind
masks of indifference

-the dating game

i want my daughter
to look at the tv
and see superheroes
who look like her
and be inspired

-not just for boys anymore

don't be afraid to fly
everything's scary
the first time

-but the views are so beautiful

sometimes
you need to be selfish
and take time
to take care
of yourself

-sometimes you need to be selfish

the only thing
you truly need
in life

is the desire
to keep going

-*keep going*

i promise you
there will be
a light
at the end
of this tunnel

-light at the end of this tunnel

i can't imagine what
you're going through

but with a hand on your
            shoulder
i tell you
i love you

-*hand on your shoulder*

you may be going
through so much pain
but remember
all scars heal
in time

-don't give up

you have so much
to live for

never forget that.

-*never forget*

keep holding on
the darkness will pass
the sun will rise
and everything will be
okay

-*everything will be okay*

i know your sorrows haunt you
and there are things
you just can't forget

but don't worry
time will pass
and you will heal

-*you will heal*

ghosts walk these halls
crying
over what could have been
while they lived

-*these halls*

the darkest times
only make sunny days
look all the brighter

-contrast

seasons change
and so does
everything else

that is our greatest blessing
and most wretched curse

-a *blessing and a curse*

drink more water today
take more time
to do your hair

show yourself
you love yourself

it's more important
than you think

-*you are important*

x

chapter three

for when you're afraid to sing

the forest would be
all too quiet
if only the birds
with the prettiest voices
sang at all

*-pearls among diamonds are still
beautiful*

you don't need someone else
to complete you

you are already complete
you are already beautiful
you are already perfect

find someone who's more
than someone to live for

find someone you want
to share life with

-someone to share life with

i dream of a future
where gender roles
don't dictate someone's life
where everyone
is treated equally

-*dream*

never tell yourself
you're not enough
because that's simply
not true

you are more than enough
and you always will be

-*more than enough*

bring down the powerful men
who abuse women
and extort sexual favors

bring them all down
for they
are truly evil

-*wicked men*

look for someone
who sees you
as the lioness
and not the cub

-*lioness*

your loneliness
will not last forever

this i promise you

your loneliness will end
even if it feels
like it never will

-*loneliness*

your cuts
are just battle scars
from wars won

for just living on
one more day
is victory enough.

-victory

you are
the universe
and all it's power
behind beautiful irises

you are everything
and nothing
will stop you

-*your power*

embrace your sexuality
sleep with who you want
or not, if you don't want to.

the choice is yours
it's your body, your life

don't let the patriarchy
hold you back
and control you

-embrace

you are not
your past mistakes

you are not
your problems

you are not
your flaws

you are
the butterfly
waiting to burst forth
from the cocoon

-*butterfly*

health care
is not a privilege

the right to keep living
and not fall into destitution
because you need care
should come
with a baby's first breath

-universal healthcare

never forget
that you
are stronger
than you think

you will overcome
every challenge

-*overcome*

being poor
does not make you
any less
of a human being

-human dignity

reaching into the mystery
into the well of life
i pulled out
something beautiful

the confidence
to know
that the path i'm taking
is the right one
and everything
will be alright.

-eternal knowledge

wilted flowers
on my dresser

i don't have the heart
to throw them out

i feel that if i do
i will be admitting
that we're over
and i just can't do that
yet

-*wilted flowers*

i want to thank
everyone who hurt me
in the past

for you only taught me
the places to kiss

on someone better

-*places to kiss*

chapter four

*for when you need to remember
who you are*

i miss
everything

about
us

-*honestly*

i just cant get you
off my mind

-*trespassing*

i've been through
many things
in my life

but nothing hurt
as much
as loving
you

-pain with the pleasure

i want to warn
everyone who comes
after me

about how much it hurts
to be loved by you
but how hard it is
to stop

-how hard it is to stop loving you

one day
you will find someone
who makes you believe
you can defeat
every monster
that comes after you

-*every monster*

the curve
of your smile
never leaves
my mind

-engraved into my mind

take me
to all
the romantic places

seduce me
in beautiful ways

i want to give you
everything

-*give you everything*

just because someone
doesn't love you back
doesn't mean
you're not
worth loving

one day
you will find someone
who sees you
and feels
that they
have just struck gold
by meeting you

-*gold*

please, don't watch me cry
i don't want you to see me
like this

-heart on my sleeve

why am i addicted
to loving
the very person
who broke me?

-*addict*

watch your friends
carefully
for signs of depression
so you can be there
for them
when they truly need it

-be there

you asked me
for a second chance
and i couldn't say no
just like every time
before

-*again and again*

i'm trying to drown
my memories of you
in whiskey

but these bastards
know how to swim

-swim

find someone
who truly understands you
and never let them go

-*never let them go*

broken souls
create
the most beautiful
art

-broken sou

don't forget
that the ones
you didn't end up with
were lost
for a reason

*-you will find your soulmate at
the right time and place*

you are not
damaged goods

don't let anyone
tell you otherwise

-*whole*

broken people
break people

-the cycle

our song comes on
and instantly
i'm in tears

remembering
all the love
and
all the heartbreak

-once again

my heart is so fragile
that
your touch
shattered it

-shattered me

all i want
is to lay with you
by the window
listening
to the rain
together

-*listening to the rain*

you are the flame
all you need
is someone
who's not afraid
to play with fire

-play with fire

there is nothing more
beautiful
to me
than the thought
of my words
building up
someone else
and encouraging them

-why i write

i may be young and foolish
but i think it's love
and there's nothing
i wont do
for you

-nothing i won't do

if a man calls you needy
just know
that he
is not enough
for you

-leave him

i want you
even though
you're bad
for me

-*desire*

you make everything
taste like sugar
and sunshine

-*my lover*

i want to get
on my knees
for you

-*on my knees*

i hope that when i die
flowers will grow on my grave
so that the world
will be made more beautiful
by my passing

-*grave*

i pray i never forget
the beauty of your face
or how good it felt
when you told me
you loved me

-*immortal words*

never go back
to those
who hurt you

if they apologize
its because
they miss what you did
for them
they don't miss
who you are

-they don't miss you

you painted my darkness
with stars

you always knew how
to turn my pain
into beauty

-*you*

you are not
the labels
they give to you

-*labels*

you have the power
to control your own fate

-*destiny*

your love
made me feel
as if i had never
been loved
before

-*something new*

i am so blessed
to wake up to your face
every morning

-*you are my sunshine*

thank you for reading. please,
please, please leave an amazon
review and post on social
media about this book- as a
self-published author, this
is my only way to get
exposure and get my
name out there. thank you!

-Amanda Everwood

27692940R00069

Made in the USA
Columbia, SC
28 September 2018